Fragments.

AND OTHER VERSE

WHERETO ARE APPENDED
THE COMPLETE POETICAL
WORKS OF
T. E. HULME

FORGOTTEN POETS

Editor: Dick Whyte   Number 3 | 2022

T.E. HULME (1883-1917) was born in Endon, a small village in the district of Staffordshire, just outside Stoke-on-Trent, in England. Hulme studied mathematics and philosophy at Cambridge, and became interested in poetry around 1907. He joined The Poets' Club in 1908, but after a disagreement left to start his own writers' circle in 1909—later dubbed the 'School of Images'—a group of experimental poets based in London, also including Edward Storer, F.S. Flint, Florence Farr, and Joseph Campbell (et al.); influenced by French *vers libre* (i.e. 'free verse'), Japanese poetic forms like *tanka* and *haikai*, and Henri Bergson's metaphysics of the 'image'. Soon abandoning poetry, Hulme wrote philosophy and art criticism for *The New Age* from 1909-1916, and worked on English translations of Bergson's *An Introduction to Metaphysics* (1912) and Georges Sorel's *Reflections on Violence* (1915). He left for WWI in 1914, and was killed in 1917 after being directly struck by a large shell. While Hulme published just 6 poems in his lifetime, his ideas were revived by the Imagists in 1913—under the leadership of Ezra Pound, and then Amy Lowell—and his work proved to be a significant forerunner to the 'new verse' movements of the 1910s.

Publication credits: Selected 'Fragments' (*The New Age*, Oct. 1921); 'Autumn' (*The Poets' Club: For Christmas MDCCCCVIII*, Jan. 1909); 'The Embankment' & 'Conversion' (*The Book of the Poets' Club*, Dec. 1909); 'Autumn', 'Mana Aboda', 'Above the Dock', 'The Embankment', & 'Conversion', published as 'The Complete Poetical Works of T.E. Hulme', in Ezra Pound's *Ripostes* (1912). To this Pound later added a few fragments abbreviated from "some of his talk made when he came home in 1915 with his first wound." (*Umbra: The Early Poems of Ezra Pound*, 1920). 'Lecture on Modern Poetry', first delivered to The Poets' Club at the end of 1908, & circulated privately; later published in Michael Roberts, *T.E. Hulme* (1938); 'Cinders' (c. 1906-7), first published posthumously in the collection of essays, *Speculations* (edited by Herbert Read, 1924).

Cover: Walter Sickert - 'Reconciliation' (*The New Age*, 1914) & 'Drawing' (*New Paths*, 1917-18); Inside: Walter Bayes - 'The Wagon', Tom Titt - 'Charing Cross', Ruth Thornhill Doggett - 'Fitzroy Square', R. Ihlee - 'Helas!', Hubert Piers - 'Dibdin's Grave', Will Dyson - 'Progess', & John P. Flanagan - 'Study' (all from *The New Age*, 1914); 'Bat Silhouette', in Harry Johnston, *British Mammals* (1903), etc.

FORGOTTEN PRESS
Aotearoa | New Zealand

ISBN: 978-1-991310-08-8 (paperback)   978-1-991310-09-5 (hardback)
978-1-991310-10-1 (ebook)

T.E. HULME
FRAGMENTS & OTHER VERSE

FRAGMENTS

Selected verses from Hulme's notebooks,
published posthumously.

"COMPLETE POEMS"

Selected verses written between 1908-1915,
first published 1912-1915.

TWO ESSAYS

'Modern Poetry' (1908) & 'Cinders' (1906-07),
published posthumously.

FORGOTTEN POETS

edited by **Dick Whyte**.

Missing Meters! Lost Lyrics!
Vanished Verses!

LEWIS ALEXANDER
PEARL ANDELSON
IRIS BARRY
GWENDOLYN BENNETT
ADELAIDE CRAPSEY
MARY CAROLYN DAVIES
HILDA DOOLITTLE
HILDEGARDE FLANNER
F.S. FLINT
JUN FUJITA
SADAKICHI HARTMANN
T.E. HULME
TAKEKO KUJO
AMY LOWELL
MINA LOY
YONE NOGUCHI
CHARLES REZNIKOFF
EDWARD STORER
MARIE TUDOR-GARLAND
AKIKO YOSHINO
AKIKO YANAGIWARA
& MANY MORE

FORGOTTENPOETS.COM

Fragments.

*Always I desire the great canvas
for my lines and gestures.*

(From the note-book of T. E. Hulme,
who was killed in the war.)

In the quiet land
There is a secret unknown fire.
Suddenly rocks shall melt
And the old roads mislead.

Across the familiar road
There is a deep cleft.
I must stand and draw back.
In the cool land
There is a secret fire.

Her head hung down
Looked fixedly at earth,
As the rabbit at the stoat,
Till she thinks the earth is the sky.

Old houses were scaffolding once,
and workmen whistling.

The bloom of the grape has gone.

That magic momentary time.

Oh God, narrow the sky,
That old star-eaten blanket,
Till it fold me round in warmth.

Somewhere the gods
(the blanket-makers in the prairie of cold)
Sleep in their blankets.

No blanket is the sky to keep warm
the little stars.

The flounced edge of skirt,
recoiling like waves off a cliff.

Down the long desolate streets of stars.

Slowly died along the scented way.

Here stand I on the pavement hard
From love's warm paradise debarred.

The mystic sadness of the sight
Of a far town seen in the night.

With a courtly bow the bent tree sighed
May I present you to my friend the sun.

At night!
All terror's in that.
Branches of the dead tree,
Silhouetted on the hill's edge.
Dark veins diseased,
On the dead white body of the sky.

The tearing iron hook
Of pitiless Mara.
Handling soft clouds in insurrection.
Brand of the obscene gods
On their flying cattle,
Roaming the sky prairie.

Sunset.

A coryphée, covetous of applause,
Loth to leave the stage,
With final diablerie, poises high her toe.
Displays scarlet lingerie of carmin'd clouds,
Amid the hostile murmurs of the stalls.

Musié.

Over a void, a desert, a flat empty space,
Came in waves, like winds,
The sound of drums, in lines,
   Sweeping like armies.
. . . . . . Dreams of soft notes
     Sail as a fleet at eve
     On a calm sea.

I lie alone in the little valley, in the noon heat,
In the kingdom of little sounds.
The hot air whispers lasciviously.
The lark sings like the sound of distant
    unattainable brooks.

As a fowl in the tall grass lies
Beneath the terror of the hawk,
The tressed white light crept
Whispering with hand on mouth mysterious
Hunting the leaping shadows in straight streets
By the white houses of old Flemish towns.

In the city square at night,
    the meeting of the torches.
The start of the great march,
The cries, the cheers, the parting.
Marching in an order
Through the familiar streets,
Through friends for the last time seen
Marching with torches.
Over the hill summit,
The moon and the moor,
And we marching alone.
The torches are out.
On the cold hill,
The cheers of the warrior dead.
(For the first time re-seen)
Marching in an order,
    To where?

The after-black lies low along the hills
Like the trailed smoke of a steamer.

Three birds flew over the red wall into
the pit of the setting sun.
O daring, doomed birds that pass
from my sight.

I walked into the wood in June
And suddenly Beauty, like a thick scented veil,
Stifled me,
Tripped me up, tight round my limbs,
Arrested me.

Far back there is a round pool,
Where trees reflected make sad memory,
Whose tense expectant surface waits
The ecstatic wave that ripples it
    In sacrament of union.

Sounds fluttered, like bats in the dusk.

Madness . . .

Four walls are round me.
I can touch them.
If I die, I can float by.

Moan and hum and remember the sea
In heaven,
    Oh my spirit,
Remember the sea and its moaning.

    Hum in the presence of God,
        it will sustain you.
Again I am cold, as after weeping.
And I tremble—but there is no wind.

the COMPLETE POETICAL
WORKS OF T. E. HULME

Beauty is the marking-time, the stationary vibration,
the feigned ecstasy of an impulse unable to
reach its natural end.

"In publishing his 'Complete Poetical Works' at thirty, Mr Hulme has set an enviable example to many of his contemporaries who have had less to say."

—EZRA POUND (1912)

AUTUMN

A touch of cold in the Autumn night—
I walked abroad,
And saw the ruddy moon lean over a hedge
Like a red-faced farmer.
I did not stop to speak, but nodded,
And round about were the wistful stars
With white faces like town children.

MANA ABODA

(unconscious mind)

Mana aboda, whose bent form
  The sky in archèd circle is,
Seems ever for an unknown grief to mourn.
Yet on a day I heard her cry:
"I weary of the roses and the singing poets—
Josephs all, not tall enough to try."

THE EMBANKMENT

Once, in finesse of fiddles found I ecstasy,
In the flash of gold heels on the
hard pavement.
Now see I
That warmth's the very stuff of poesy.
Oh, God, make small
The old star-eaten blanket of the sky,
That I may fold it round me and in
comfort lie.

ABOVE THE DOCK

Above the quiet dock in mid night,
Tangled in the tall mast's corded height,
Hangs the moon. What seemed so far away
Is but a child's balloon, forgotten after play.

CONVERSION

Lighthearted I walked into the valley wood
   In the time of hyacinths,
Till beauty like a scented cloth
Cast over, stifled me. I was bound
Motionless and faint of breath
By loveliness that is her own eunuch.

Now pass I to the final river
Ignominiously, in a sack, without sound,
As any peeping Turk to the Bosphorus.

POEM

Abbreviated from the Conversation of Mr. T.E.H.

Over the flat slope of St. Eloi
 A wide wall of sandbags.
Night,
In the silence desultory men
Pottering over small fires,
    cleaning their mess-tins:
To and fro, from the lines,
Men walk as on Piccadilly,
Making paths in the dark,
Through scattered dead horses,
Over a dead Belgian's belly.

The Germans have rockets.
The English have no rockets.

Behind the lines, cannon, hidden,
Lying back miles.
Before the line, chaos:

My mind is a corridor.
The minds about me are corridors.

Nothing suggests itself.
There is nothing to do but keep on.

ESSAYS

T. E. HULME

LECTURE ON MODERN POETRY
T. E. HULME
[abridged]

*I want to speak of verse
in a plain way as I would of pigs:
that is the only honest way.*

I have no reverence for tradition. I came to the subject of verse from the inside rather than from the outside. There were certain impressions which I wanted to fix. I read verse to find models, but I could not find any that seemed exactly suitable to express that kind of impression... until I came to French vers-libre, which seemed to exactly fit the case.

The new technique was first definitely stated by Kahn. It consisted in a denial of a regular number of syllables as the basis of versification. The length of the line is long and short, oscillating with the images used by the poet; it follows the contours of their thoughts and is free rather than regular; to use a rough analogy, it is clothes made to order, rather than ready-made clothes. This is a very bald statement of it, and I am not concerned here so much with French poetry as with English. The kind of verse I advocate is not the same as vers-libre, I merely use the French as an example of the extraordinary effect that an emancipation of verse can have on poetic activity.

The ancient Greeks were perfectly aware of the fluidity of the world and of its impermanence; there was the Greek theory that the whole world was a flux. But while they recognized it, they feared it and endeavoured to evade it, to construct things of permanence which would stand fast in this universal flux which frightened them. They had the disease, the passion, for immortality. They wished to construct things which should be proud boasts that they, men, were immortal. Materially in [their architecture], spiritually in the dogmas of religion and in the hypostatized ideas of Plato. Living in a dynamic world they wished to create a static fixity where their souls might rest.

This I conceive to be the explanation of many of the old ideas on poetry. They wish to embody in a few lines a perfection of thought. Of the thousand and one ways in which a thought might roughly be conveyed to a hearer there was one way which was the perfect way, which was destined to embody that thought to all eternity, hence the fixity of the form of poem and the elaborate rules of regular metre. It was to be an immortal thing and the infinite pains taken to fit a thought into a fixed and artificial form are necessary and understandable.

Now the whole trend of the modern spirit is away from that; philosophers no longer believe in absolute truth. We no longer believe in perfection, either in verse or in thought, we frankly acknowledge the relative. We shall no longer strive to attain the absolutely perfect form in poetry. Instead of these minute perfections of phrase and words, the tendency will be rather towards the production of a general effect; this of course takes away the predominance of metre and a regular number of syllables as the element of perfection in words. We are no longer concerned that stanzas shall be shaped and polished like gems, but rather that some vague mood shall be communicated.

The criticism is sure to be made, what is this new spirit, which finds itself unable to express itself in the old metre? Are the things that a poet wishes to say now in any way different to the things that former poets say? I believe that they are. The old poetry dealt essentially with big things, the expression of epic subjects leads naturally to the anatomical matter and regular verse. Action can best be expressed in regular verse.

But the modern is the exact opposite of this, it no longer deals with heroic action, it has become definitely and finally introspective and deals with expression and communication of momentary phases in the poet's mind... The opinion you often hear expressed, that perhaps a new poet will arrive who will synthesize the whole modern movement into a great epic, shows an entire misconception of the tendency of modern verse.

There is an analogous change in painting, where the old endeavoured to tell a story, the modern attempts to fix an impression. We still perceive the mystery of things, but we perceive it in entirely a different way—no longer directly in the form of action, but as an impression... What has found expression in painting as Impressionism will soon find expression in poetry as 'free verse'.

Say the poet is moved by a certain landscape, they select from that certain images which, put into juxtaposition in separate lines, serve to suggest and to evoke the state they feel. To this piling-up and juxtaposition of distinct images in different lines, one can find a fanciful analogy in music. A great revolution in music when, for the melody that is one-dimensional, was substituted harmony which moves in two. Two visual images form what one may call a visual chord. They unite to suggest an image which is different to both.

The criticism is sure to be made that when you have abolished the regular syllabled line as the unit of poetry, you have turned it into prose. Of course this is perfectly true of a great quantity of modern verse. In fact, one of the great blessings of the abolition of regular metre would be that it would at once expose all this sham poetry. Poetry as an abstract thing is a very different matter, and has its own life, quite apart from metre as a convention.

To test the question of whether it is possible to have poetry written without a regular metre, I propose to pick out one great difference between the two. I don't profess to give an infallible test that would enable anyone to at once say: 'This is, or is not, true poetry', but it will be sufficient for the purposes of this paper. It is this: that there are, roughly speaking, two methods of communication, a direct, and a conventional language. The direct language is poetry, it is direct because it deals in images. The indirect language is prose, because it uses images that have died and become figures of speech. The difference between the two is, roughly, this: that while one arrests your mind all the time with a picture, the other allows the mind to run along with the least possible effort to a conclusion.

Prose is due to a faculty of the mind something resembling reflex action in the body. If I had to go through a complicated mental process each time I laced my boots, it would waste mental energy; instead of that, the mechanism of the body is so arranged that one can do it almost without thinking. It is an economy of effort. The same process takes place with the images used in prose. For example, when I say that the hill was clad with trees, it merely conveys the fact to me that it was covered. But the first time that expression was used was by a poet, and to them it was an image recalling... the distinct visual analogy of someone clad in clothes; but the image has died. One might say that images are born in poetry. They are used in prose, and finally die a long, lingering death in journalists' English. Now this process is very rapid, so that the poet must continually be creating new images, and their sincerity may be measured by the number of their images.

One might sum it all up in this way: a shell is a very suitable covering for the egg at a certain period of its career, but very unsuitable at a later age. This seems to me to represent fairly well the state of verse at the present time. While the shell remains the same, the inside character is entirely changed. It is not addled, as a pessimist might say, but has become alive, it has changed from the ancient art of [regular verse] to the modern impressionist, but the mechanism of verse has remained the same. It can't go on doing so. I will conclude, ladies and gentlemen, by saying,

the shell must be broken.

CINDERS

A PREFACE BY THE AUTHOR

The history of the philosophers we know, but who will write the history of the philosophic amateurs and readers? Who will tell us of the circulation of Descartes, who read the book and who understood it? Or do philosophers, like the mythical people on the island, take in each other's washing? Are they the only readers of each other's books? For I take it, a man who understands philosophy is inevitably irritated into writing it. The few who have learnt the jargon must repay themselves by employing it. A new philosophy is not like a new religion, a thing to be merely thankful for and accepted mutely by the faithful. It is more of the nature of food thrown to the lions; the pleasure lies in the fact that it can be devoured. It is food for the critics, and all readers of philosophy, I suppose, are critics, and not faithful ones waiting for the new gospel.

With this preface I offer my new kind of food to tickle the palate of the connoisseurs.

CINDERS

T. E. HULME

From a Bronze by Jacob Epstein.

CINDERS

A Sketch of a New Weltanschauung

(c. 1906-7)

I. In spite of pretensions to absolute truth, the results of philosophy are always tested by the effects, and by the judgements of other philosophers. There is always an appeal to a circle of people. The same is true of values in art, in morals. Humans cannot stand on absolute ground, but always appeals to their fellows.

II. Therefore it is suggested that there is no such thing as an 'absolute truth' to be discovered. All general statements about truth, etc., are in the end only amplifications of our appetites.

The ultimate reality is a circle of persons, i.e. animals who communicate.

There is a kind of gossamer web, woven between the real things, and by this means the animals communicate. For purposes of communication they invent a symbolic language. Afterwards this language, used to excess, becomes a disease, and we get the curious phenomena of humans explaining themselves by means of the gossamer web that connects them. Language becomes a disease in the hands of the counter-word mongers. It must constantly be remembered that it is an invention for the convenience of humans; and in the midst of Hegelians who triumphantly explain the world as a mixture of 'Good' and 'Beauty' and 'Truth', this should be remembered. What would an intelligent animal (without the language disease), or a carter in the road, think of it all? Symbols are picked out and believed to be realities. People imagine that all the complicated structure of the world can be woven out of 'good' and 'beauty'. These words are merely counters representing vague groups of things, to be moved about on a board for the convenience of the players.

III. Objection might be taken that this makes humans the measure of the world, and that after all we are only an animal, who came late, and the world must be supposed to have existed before we evolved at all. The reply to this is as follows... The mental qualities of people and animals are common, though they are reached ny different means.

IV. Just as no common purpose can be aimed at for the conflicting purposes of real people, so there is no common purpose in the world.

The world is a plurality.

A unity arrived at by stripping off essentials is not a unity. Compound is not an inner reality.

V. This plurality consists in the nature of an ash-heap. In this ash-pit of cinders, certain ordered routes have been made, thus constituting whatever unity there may be—a kind of manufactured chess-board laid on a cinder-heap. Not a real chess-board impressed on the cinders, but the gossamer world of symbolic communication already spoken of.

CINDERS
[excerpts]

There is a difficulty in finding a comprehensive scheme of the cosmos, because there is none. The cosmos is only *organised* in parts; the rest is cinders.

Death is a breaking up into cinders. Hence partial truth of the old Greek conception of Hades (a place of less organisation and no happiness).

Many necessary conditions must be fulfilled before the counters and the chess-board can be posed elegantly on the cinders. Illness and death easily disturb and give falls from this condition. Perhaps this is an illustration of Nietzsche's image of the tight-rope walker. When all is arranged the counters are moved about. This is happiness, moving to enthusiastic conclusions, the musical note, perhaps Art. But it must be largely artificial. (Art prolongs it, and creates it by blur.)

The floating heroic world (built up of moments) and the cindery reality—can they be made to correspond to some fundamental constitution of the world? (An antithesis much more deep than the one which analyses all realities into forms of egoism. This latter only a particular case of the general law.)

The *absolute* is to be described not as perfect, but if existent as essentially imperfect, chaotic, and cinder-like. (Even this view is not ultimate, but merely designed to satisfy temporary human analogies and wants.)

World is indescribable, that is, not reducible to counters; and particularly it is impossible to include it all under one large counter such as 'God' or 'Truth' and the other verbalisms, or the disease of the symbolic language.

Cinders can never be counters except for certain practical purposes (good enough)—*cf.* rail lines and chess-board. The treatment of the soul as the central part of the nominalist position. Their habit of regarding it as a kind of round counter all red, which survives *whole* in all its redness and roundness (the redness as the character), a counter-like *distinct* separate entity, just as *word* itself is.

Why is it that London looks pretty by night? Because for the general cindery chaos there is substituted a simple ordered arrangement of a finite number of lights.

The two complementary phenomena: that each wash is a line, and that each line is a wash.

That the world is finite (atomism: there are no

infinitudes except in art) and that it is yet an infinitude of cinders (there is no finite law encompassing all).

This new view may perhaps be caricatured by saying that the bad is fundamental, and that the good is artificially built up in it and out of it, like oases in the desert, or as cheerful houses in the storm.

(Two parts: 1—All cinders; 2—the part built up. So the question: How far built up and how far given us? The question of the pliability of the world.)

All is flux. The moralists, the capital letterists, attempt to find a framework outside the flux, a solid bank for the river, a pier rather than a raft. Truth is what helps a particular sect in the general flow.

School children at a fountain (moved mechanically by thirst) to someone looking down from above, appear as a pure instinctive mechanical act. *Cf.* ants— we are unable to ascertain the subtler reasons which move them. They all look alike. Hence humpty-dumpty's remark about human faces is seen to be the foundation of all science and all philosophy.

Only in the fact of consciousness is there a unity in the world, cf. Oxford Street at 2 A.M. All the mud, endless, except where bound together by the spectator.

Unity is made in the world by drawing squares

over it. We are able to get along these at any rate—*cf.*
railway line in desert. (Always the elusive as seen in
maps. *Ad infinitum.*)

The squares include cinders—always cinders.

No unity of laws, but merely of the sorting
machine.

Formerly, one liked theories because they
reduced the world to a single principle. Now the same
reason disgusts us. The flats of Canada are
incomprehensible on any single theory. The world
only comprehensible on the cinder theory.

The same old fallacy persists—the desire to
introduce a unity in the world: (1) The mythologists
made it a woman or an elephant; (2) The scientists
made fun of the mythologists, but themselves turned
the world into the likeness of a mechanical toy. They
were more concerned with models than with woman
(woman troubled them and hence their particular
form of anthropomorphism). One analogy is as good
as another. The truth remains that the world is not any
unity, but a house in the cinders (outside in the cold,
primeval).

Contrast the Pythagorean ecstasies in the
numbers 3 and 7. The cinder is the opposite prejudice.
I am immediately up in arms if a book says a subject
can be divided into three separate parts.

Most of our life is spent in buttoning and

unbuttoning. Yes, quite so. This fact can be welcomed as fitting in with the general theory.

The unity of Nature is an extremely artificial and fragile bridge, a garden net.

The covers of a book are responsible for much error. They set a limit round certain convenient groups of ideas, when there are really no limits.

The aim of science and of all thought is to reduce the complex and inevitably disconnected world of grit and cinders to a few ideal counters, which we can move about and so form an ungritlike picture of reality—one flattering to our sense of power over the world.

In the end this is true too of mathematics, though at first it appears as a more complex symbolism. The conclusion of all mathematics is: That one counter stands in a certain relation to another. That counter may be a simple number or an elliptic integral, but the final effect is the same. (All mathematics is deducible from numbers, which are nothing but counters.)

There is an *objective* world (?), a chaos, a cinder-heap. Gradually oases have been built up. Egos have grown as organised trees.

So not *idealist*, as that assumes that there is

nothing but a fixed number of persons, and without them nothing. (So the Real New Realism is something beyond names. World can't be O because O is opposed to human psychology.)

A landscape, with occasional oases. So now and then we are moved—at the theatre, action, a love. But mainly deserts of dirt, ash-pits of the cosmos, grass on ash-pits. No universal ego, but a few definite persons gradually built up.

Nature as the accumulation of the memories of humans.

Certain groups of ideas as huts for humans to live in. The Act of Creation.

Truth is always seen to lie in a compromise. All clear cut ideas turn out to be wrong. Analogy to real things, which are artificially picked out of the general lava flow of cinders.

Cf. The wandering attention in the library. Sometimes one seems to have definite clear cut moments, but not afterwards.

I. Nature. Scenery as built up by humans. Oases in the desert of grit.

II. Extended to the whole of the world.

III. *But* the microscope. Things revealed, not created, but there before, and *also* seem to be in an order.

IV. Before humans other powers created in the struggle.

V. So humans were gradually built up, and the 'human' world was gradually built up at the same time.

Evolution of colour; dim perception of it in the amoeba; evolved—the whole modern world of colour built up from this; gradually made more counter-like and distinct.

There is no inevitable order into which ideas must be shifted.

We live in a room, of course, but the great question for philosophy is: how far have we decorated the room, and how far was it made before we came? Did we merely decorate the room, or did we make it from chaos? The laws of nature that we certainly do find—what are they?

In an organised city it is not easy to see the cinder element of earth—all is banished. But it is easy to see it psychologically. What the Nominalists call the grit in the machine, I call the fundamental element of the machine.

Properly to estimate the true purpose of absolute philosophy, it should be realised as reducing everything to number, the only rational and logical solution from the point of view that dares to conceive relation as of more importance than the persons related.

The eyes, the beauty of the world, have been organised out of the faces. Humans return to dust. So does the face of the world to primeval cinders.

Only the isolated points seem to have any value, so how can the world be said to be designed? Rather we may say that gradually certain points are being designed.

Taken *mystically* then all peculiarities of the human organ-ism must have their counter-part in the construction of the world.

E.g. Illness and a reversion to chaos.

Humans are the chaos highly organised, but liable to revert to chaos at any moment. Happiness and ecstasy at present unstable . . .

The two moods in life, (i) Ill in bed, toothache—the disorganised, withdrawn-into-oneself mood, (ii) Flying along in the wind (wind in the hair, on a motor bus). *Or* evolving a new theory. The impersonal feeling.

Ennui and disgust, the sick moments—not an occasional lapse or disease, but the fundamental ennui and chaos out of which the world has been built, and which is as necessary to it as the listeners are to intellectuals. The old world order of queens and pawns.

The apparent scientific unity of the world may be due to the fact that humans are a kind of sorting machine.

"I must tell someone" as the final criterion of philosophy, the *raison d'etre* of the human circle symbol.

The sick disgusting moments are part of the fundamental cinders—primeval chaos—the dream of impossible chaos.

The absolute is invented to reconcile conflicting purposes. But these purposes are necessarily conflicting, even in the nature of Truth itself. It is so absurd to construct an absolute which shall at each moment just manage by artificial gymnastics to reconcile these purposes.

Philosophical syntheses and ethical systems are only possible in arm-chair moments. They are seen to be meaningless as soon as we get into a bus with a dirty baby and a crowd.

Note the fact that all a writer's generalisations and truths can be traced to the personal circumstances and prejudices of their class, experience, capacity and body. This, however, is not an instance of error or hypocrisy. There is no average or real truth to be discerned among the different fronts of prejudice.

Each is a truth in so far as it satisfies the writer.

We must judge the world from the status of animals, leaving out 'Truth', etc.

Animals are in the same state that humans were before symbolic language was invented.

Philosophy is about people in clothes, not about the 'soul of man'.

The fixed order of the world is woven in a gigantic way by the acts of humans and animals.

The world lives in order to develop the lines on its face.

These little theories of the world, which satisfy and are then thrown away, one after the other, develop *not* as successive approximations to the truth, but like successive thirsts, to be satisfied at the moment, and not evolving to one great Universal Thirst.

Through all the ages, the conversation of ten men sitting together is what holds the world together.

Never think in a book: here are Truth and all the other capital letters; but think in a theatre and watch the audience. Here is the reality, here are human animals. Listen to the words of heroism and then at the crowded husbands who applaud. All philosophies are subordinate to this. It is not a question of the unity of the world and humans afterwards put into it, but of human animals, and of philosophies as an elaboration of their appetites.

Words.

Heaven as the short summary paradise of words.

The ideal of knowledge: all cinders reduced to counters (words); these counters moved about on a chess-board, and so all phenomena made obvious.

Something is always lost in generalisation. A railway leaves out all the gaps of dirt between. Generalisations are only means of getting about. *Cf.* the words love, sex, nude, with the actual details.

I hate more than anything vague long pretentious words... "indefinable tendency in events" etc., etc.

Always seek the hard, definite, personal word.

The real levelheadedness: to... be able to imagine the effect of dipping in water—this is what one must be able to do for words, and for all embracing philosophies. We must not be taken in by the arm-chair moments.

The World is Round.

Disillusionment comes when it is recognised that all heroic actions can be reduced to the simple laws of egoism. But wonder can even then be found in the fact that there are such different and clear-cut laws and egoisms and that they have been created out of the chaos.

The pathetic search for the different. Where shall they find it ? Never found in sex. All explored sex is the same.

World as finite, and so no longer any refuge in infinities of grandeur.

Atomism.

Resolution of apparent flexibility and continuity into atomic structure. Oratory and fluency mean a collection of phrases at fingers' ends. This seen in Hyde Park, the young men, Christian preachers.
Escapes to the infinite:
(i) Art. Blur, strangeness, music.
(ii) Sentimentality.

The sentimental illusion of a man (invalid) who takes pleasure in resting his head in a woman's lap—it is a deliberate act, work on her part. While he may feel the sentimental escape to the infinite, she has to be uncomfortable and prosaic.

All experience tends to do away with all sentimental escapes to the infinite, but at the same time to provide many deliberated, observed, manufactured, artificial, spectacular, poised for seeing continuities and patterns.

The universal conspiracy: other people unconsciously provide the sentimental spectacle in which you luxuriate. The world is nothing more or less than a stage.

There may be an attitude which sees that most things are illusions, that experience is merely the gradual process of disillusionment, that the new as well as the old ideals turn out to be partial, non-continuous or infinite, but then in face of this decides that certain illusions or moods are pleasurable and exhilarating, and deliberately and knowingly encourages them. A judicious choice of illusions, leading to activities planned and carried out, is the only means of happiness, *e.g.* the exhilaration of regarding life as a procession or a war.

In opposition to socialism and Utopian schemes comes the insistence on the fact of the unalterability of motives. Motives are the only unalterable and fixed things in the world. They extend to the animal kingdom. They are the only rock: physical bases change. They are more than human motives: they are the constitution of the world.

That great secret which all people find out for themselves, and none reveal or if they do, like Cassandra, are not believed—that the world is round. The young man refuses to believe it.

Refuse World as a unit and take Person (in flight from the word fallacy).

But why person? Why is the line drawn exactly there in the discussion of counter words?

We are becoming so particular in the choice of words and the rejection of symbolisms that we are in danger of forgetting that the world does really exist.

The truth is that there are no ultimate principles, upon which the whole of knowledge can be built once and for ever as upon a rock. But there are an infinity of analogues, which help us along, and give us a feeling of power over the chaos when we perceive them. The field is infinite and herein lies the chance for originality. Here there are some new things under the sun. (Perhaps it would be better to say that there are some new things under the moon, for here is the land pre-eminently of shadows, fancies and analogues.)

Danger.

One must recognise thought's essential in-dependence of the imagery that steadies it. Subtle associations which familiar images recall are insinuated into the thought.

Though perhaps we do not realise it, we are still governed by the analogy, by which spirit was first compared to the wind. The contrast the same as the one between the little box and space, between the court and cinders—that between the one that thinks of a 'human' as an elaborately built up pyramid, a constructed elaboration, easily upset and not flexible, only functioning in one direction, the one in which it was made, and the other that considers us as having a flexible essence, a spirit, like a *fluid*.

We can all see that there is an eternal flexibility in the most obviously constituted man, but we realise the contrast best when looking at a tailor's model of a man in dress, whose limbs move and flex.

In the problem of ghosts which bend and flex lies the whole difference between the two world philosophies—

I. Flexible essence.
II. Built up stuff.

Philosophical Jargon.

There is this consoling thought, supporting us while wandering in the wilderness of which the priests alone pretend they have the secret. In all other uses of language, no matter for what purpose, the analogies used are quite simple, and even can be replaced, leaving the idea behind them just as real. The analogies a person uses to represent a state of soul, though personal, can be replaced, to produce almost the same effect. No one mistakes the analogies for the real thing they stand for.

The Dancer.

Dancing to express the organisation of cinders, finally emancipated (*cf.* Birds).

I sat before a stage and saw a little girl with her head thrown back, and a smile. I knew her, for she was the daughter of John of Elton... But she smiled, and her feet were not like feet, but . . .

All these sudden insights... all of these start a line, which seems about to unite the whole world logically. But the line stops. There is no unity. All logic and life are made up of tangled ends like that.

Always think of the fringe and of the cold walks, of the lines that lead nowhere.

Mind and Matter.

Realise that to take *one* or the *other* as absolute is to perpetrate the same old counter fallacy; both are mixed up in a cindery way and we extract them as counters.

Mathematics takes one group of counters,

abstracts them and makes them absolute, down to Matter and Motion.

That fringe of cinders which bounds any ecstasy.

The tall lanky person, with a rose, in a white moonlit field. But where do they sleep?

All heroes... go to the outside, away from the Room, and wrestle with cinders.

And cinders become the Azores, the Magic Isles.

A house built is then a symbol, a Roman Viaduct; but the walk there and the dirt—this must jump right into the mind also.

Aphra's Finger.

There are moments when the tip of one's finger seems raw. In the contact of it and the world there seems a strange difference. The spirit lives on that tip and is thrown on the rough cinders of the world. All philosophy depends on that—the state of the tip of the finger.

When Aphra had touched, even lightly, the rough wood, this wood seemed to cling to his finger, to draw itself backward and forward along it. The spirit returned again and again, as though fascinated, to the luxurious torture of the finger.

The prediction of the stars is no more wonderful, and no more accurate than the prediction of another person's conduct. There is no last refuge here for the logical structure of the world.

The phenomenon we study is not the immense world in our hand, but certain little observations we make about it. We put these on a table and look at them.

We study little chalk marks on a table (chalk because that shows the cindery nature of the division we make) and create rules near enough for them.

If we look at a collection of cinders from all directions, in the end, we are bound to find a shadow that looks regular.

The attempt to get a common element in personality, i.e. the old attempt to get a unity. Abstract an element and call that a fundamental.

The inner spirit of the world is miles and miles of ploughed fields.

Never speak of 'my unconquerable soul' or of any vulgarism of that sort. But thank God for the long note of the bugle, which moves all the world bodily out of the cinders and the mud.

There is only one art that moves me: architecture.

The Eagle's Eye.

The ruling analogy, which is quite false, must be

removed. It is that of the eagle's eye. The metaphysician imagines that they survey the world as with an eagle's eye. And the farther they fly, the 'purer' their knowledge becomes.

Hence we can see the world as pure geometry, and can make out its dividing lines.

But the eye is in the mud, the eye is mud.

Pure seeing of the whole process is impossible, little fancies help us along, but we never get pure disinterested intellect.

Space.

I. Admitted the pragmatic criterion of any analogy that makes for clearness.

II. Now space is essential to clearness. A developed notion, perhaps, but now essential.

III. The idealists analyse space into a mode of arranging sensations. But this gives us an unimaginable world existing all at a point.

IV. Why not try the reverse process and put all ideas (purely mental states) into terms of space (*cf.* landscape thinking)?

The sense of reality is inevitably connected with that of space (the world existing before us).

Truths don't exist before we invent them. They respond to the human need of economy, just as beliefs to their need of faith.

The fountain turned on. It has a definite geometrical shape, but the shape did not exist before it was turned on. Compare the arguments about the pre-existence of the soul.

But the little pipes are there before, which give it that shape as soon the water is turned on.

The water is the same though the geometrical figures of different fountains differ.

By analogy we may perhaps claim that there is no such thing as a personal soul. The personality of the soul depends on the bodily frame which receives it, i.e. on the shape of the pipes.

The soul is a spirit certainly, but undifferentiated and without personality. The personality is given by the bodily frame which receives and shapes it.

Ritual and sentiment.

Sentiment cannot easily retire into itself in pure thought; it cannot live and feed on itself for very long. In wandering, thought is easily displaced by other matters. So that the person who deliberately sets themself the task of thinking continuously of a lover or dead friend has an impossible task. They are inevitably drawn to some form of ritual for the expression and outflow of the sentiment. Some act which requires less concentration, and which at an easy level fulfills their obligations to sentiment, which changes a morbid feeling into a grateful task and employment.

Such as pilgrimages to graves, standing bare-headed and similar freaks of a lover's fancy. The same phenomena can be observed in religion. A person cannot deliberately make up their mind to think of the goodness of God for an hour, but they can perform some ritual act of admiration whether it be the offering of a sacrifice or merely saying amen to a set prayer. Ritual tends to be constant, even that seeming exception the impromptu prayers of a Non-conformist minister are merely the stringing together in accidental order of set and well-known phrases and tags. The burning of candles to the Virgin if only one can escape from some danger. The giving of a dinner, or getting drunk in company as a celebration, a relief from concentrated thinking.

Body.

In the lift hearing the phrase 'fed up', and realising that all our analogies spiritual and intellectual are derived from purely physical acts. Nay more, all attributes of the absolute and the abstract are really nothing more (in so far as they mean anything) but elaborations of simple passions.

All poetry is an affair of the body—that is, to be

real it must affect body.

Action.

Just as sentiment and religion require expression in ritual, so tragedy requires action.

Jealousy, desire to kill, desire for strong arms and knives, resolution to shake off social convention and to do it. The knife order.

Why grumble because there is no end discoverable in the world? There is no end at all except in our own constructions.

Necessity of distinguishing between a vague philosophic statement that "reality always escapes a system" and the definite cinder, felt in a religious way and being a criterion of nearly all judgment, philosophic and aesthetic.

No Geist [*spirit*] without ghost.
This the only truth in the subject.

Is there here a possible violation of the cinder principle; an escape back to the old fallacy? But without some definite assertion of this kind... Some definite crossing beyond is necessary to escape poetic over-statement, to relieve us.

Philosophy.

The strange quality, shade of feeling, one gets (a few people alone in a position a little separated from the world); a ship's cabin, the last bus.

If all the world were destroyed and only these left. . . . That all the gods, all the winged words (love . . .) exist in them on that fluid basis.

To take frankly that fluid basis and elaborate it into a solidity, that the gods do not exist horizontally in space but somehow vertically in the isolated fragment of the tribe. There is another form of space where gods, etc., do exist concretely.

Smoothness.

Hate it.
This is the obsession that starts all my theories.
Get other examples, other facets of the one idea.
Build them up by catalogue method;
    (I) in science;
    (II) in sex;
    (III) in poetry.

Analogy.

I look at the reality, at London stream, and dirt, mud, power, and then I think of the pale shadowy analogy that is used without thinking by the automatic philosophers, the 'stream of time'. The people who treat words without reverence, who use analogies without thinking of them: let us always remember that solid real stream and the flat thin voice of the metaphysician, 'the stream of time'.

Extended clay. Looking at the Persian Gulf on a map and imagining the mud shore at night.

Pictures of low coasts of any country. We are all just above the sea.

Delight in perceiving the real cinder construction in a port. Upon mud as distinct from the clear-cut harbour on the map . . .

Must see these different manifestations of the cinders; otherwise we cannot work the extended clay.

A melancholy spirit, the mind like a great desert lifeless, and the sound of march music in the street, passes like a wave over that desert, unifies it, but then goes.

Valet to the Absolute.

The exact fault: the taking of a few opinions, a few epigrams, a few literary *obiter dicta*, and arranging them symmetrically, finding a logical order, an underlying principle where there is one, and calling the whole a science.

I shall call my philosophy the 'Valet to the Absolute'. The Absolute not a hero to its own valet.

All these various little notes will never combine because in their nature they cannot. The facts of Nature are solid enough, but Humans are a weathercock standing in the middle, looking first at one part and then at another. A little idea in one sentence appears to contain a whole new world philosophy. So it does. But then a world philosophy is only a certain direction, N. or S. It is quite easy to change this direction. Hence the astonishing power that philosophers appear to have at the summit of the sciences. Buy a book obviously literary, by an amateur, made of light combinations of words. It seems to change the world, but nothing is further from the truth. It just turns the weathercock to a new direction. The philosophic faculty is quite irresponsible, the easiest moving thing in nature, and quite divorced from nature.

So be sceptical of the first enthusiasm that a new idea gives.

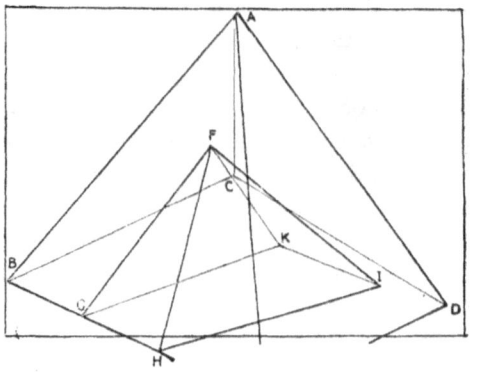

This Space for Your Thoughts

THE OLD EXPRESSIONS ARE WITH US ALWAYS
AND THERE ARE ALWAYS OTHERS

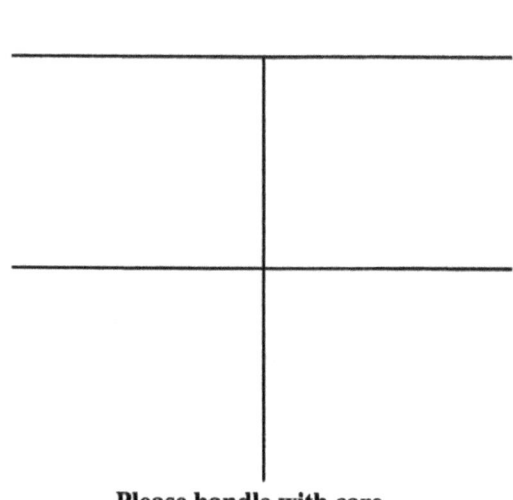

Please handle with care.